W9-DCL-833

WHAT IS? SERIES: VOLUME 1
WHAT IS COLLEGE?

BY: HENRY KECULAH JR.

Copyright © 2020 by 4.0 GPA LLC.
All rights reserved. Published by 4.0 GPA LLC, 2700 Post Oak Blvd,
21st Floor, Houston, TX 77056
Printed in the U.S.A

Library of Congress Control Number: 2020940095

DEDICATED TO MY CLOSE FRIEND AND COLLEGE
ROOMMATE, UCHECHUKWU C. DIRIBE.

1989 - 2016

Uche: Hey, BJ; my name is Uche! Nice to meet you, bro.
BJ: Hi! I am new to Alief; my family moved from Euless.
Uche: You'll enjoy Alief! I'm excited to be a fifth-grader.
BJ: I like your first name, where does that come from?
Uche: My family is from Nigeria, which is located in Africa.
BJ: My mom is Liberian, and my dad is Jamaican. Both of my grandparents are born on July 25th!
Uche: I love Alief. Besides, it is very **diverse**. My birthday is on July 8th. That is very cool, BJ.

BJ: Yesterday, I was watching a basketball game on TV, and I saw a commercial talking about **college**. Uche, do you know anything about **college**?

Uche: I know a lot about colleges; both of my parents went to **college**.

BJ: Can I go to **college**, too, even though neither of my parents went?

Uche: Yes, of course, you can! You can still go to **college**, even if no one in your family has attended it before.

BJ: What can I do to increase my chances of going to **college**?

Uche: Well, I heard that if you pay attention to the teacher and do all your homework, you will perform well in **college**.

BJ: You mean, I need to stop talking in class when the teacher talks?

Uche: Yes, exactly. If you listen to the teacher and do all of your homework, you'll probably do well on your **ACT** and **SAT** exams, too.

BJ: **ACT** and **SAT** exams? What are those?

Uche: **ACT** stands for American **College** Testing, and it's a standardized test that colleges use for future students. **SAT** stands for Scholastic Assessment Test, which is another test students can take to be admitted to **college**. These two exams test you on many subjects, like English, writing, science, and math. That's why I'm telling you, BJ; you have to pay attention to all of your classes to be better prepared for these exams.

BJ: So, wait. If I don't try hard in my classes now, that could affect me in the future? But what if I just want to play basketball? I don't really need **college** if all I want to do is go to the NBA, right?

Uche: The thing is, BJ, everything you learn in school, from the first through to the twelfth grade, will help you get into **college**. And even basketball players need good grades to play sports in **college**. Did you know that if you don't take the **ACT** or **SAT**, you can't play basketball in **college**? BJ, all you have to do is stop talking when the teacher is teaching and do all your homework.

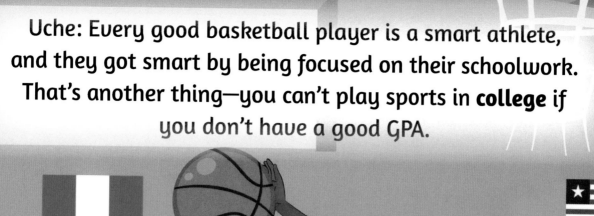

Uche: Every good basketball player is a smart athlete, and they got smart by being focused on their schoolwork. That's another thing—you can't play sports in **college** if you don't have a good GPA.

BJ: What is a **GPA**?

Uche: GPA stands for grade point average. It works similar to the report cards we get now.

For example an A = 4.0

B = 3.0

C = 2.0

D = 1.0

F = 0.0

You add all the points together and divide the results by the number of classes you have.

This is my report card from last year. I took four classes. I made an A in math, A in science, A in English, and a B in social studies. I add 4+4+4+3, which equals 15 points. Now I divide the 15 by 4 because that's how many classes I have. The answer equals 3.75. My GPA for that period would have been 3.75.

BJ: Is that a good GPA?

Uche: Yes, anything above a 3.00 is a relatively good GPA.

REPORT CARD

Class	Grade	GPA Value
		4.0
	A 94	4.0
Math	A 92	4.0
Science	A 96	3.0
English	B 85	
Social Studies		

Total GPA: = 3.75

BJ: Do we have GPAs right now?

Uche: We have GPAs in high school. Some middle school students who take high school courses will have a GPA when they start high school

BJ: That is very good information. I am always playing NBA 2K and video games, but I need to start taking education more seriously. I want to have a high GPA in high school.

Uche: My older sister received a scholarship to **college** because her GPA was 3.88. Now she gets to attend **college** for free and avoid taking out loans.

BJ: You have to pay for **college** as well? Is it not free, like our school?

Uche: Yes, **college** is costly! Most schools cost $10,000 or more a year. But don't get discouraged. There are scholarship opportunities out there for academics and athletics.

BJ: Did Kevin Durant pay to attend the University of Texas at Austin, or did he go for free?

Uche: Kevin Durant received an athletic scholarship because he was a good athlete and met the NCAA's GPA requirement to play sports in sports in **college**.

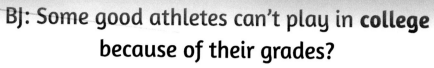

BJ: Some good athletes can't play in **college** because of their grades?
Uche: Yes, some of the best athletes do not play in **college** because they are **ineligible**, and their GPAs are too low.

"Let's Be Great"

16

BJ: I want to go to **college** even more now.

Uche: People who graduate from **college** earn a million dollars more during their life than people who only graduated from high school.

BJ: I heard my cousins talk about how bad student loan debt is, and I was like, "I don't want that debt stuff."

Uche: Education is an investment. If you pay attention now, you will not have a lot of debt. There are several benefits to attending **college**, as well.

BJ: What are some of the benefits of attending **college**?

Uche: You can obtain a job that earns you more money. **College** allows you to build your network and learn stuff that will help you as an adult.

BJ: Uche, you have changed my **perspective** on **college**.

Uche: **College** allows you to select a subject you want to major in.

BJ: What do you mean by major in?

Uche: If you like math, you can major in math.

BJ: I want to be on TV and be a news reporter like Isiah Carey. What do I major in?

Uche: You would major in **journalism**. Mr. Carey attended **Southern University and A&M College** in Baton Rouge. **Southern University and A&M College** is considered an **HBCU**.

BJ: My favorite rapper, Lil Baby, did not go to **college**, and he makes a lot of money.

Uche: Have you heard of the word "probability"?

BJ: What does that mean?

Uche: Probability is a strong likelihood or chance something will happen. There are not many successful rappers like Lil Baby. You also have great rappers like J. Cole, Ludacris, David Banner, Childish Gambino, and Sage Francis, who have **college** degrees.

BJ: I never knew rappers went to **college** and got degrees!

BJ: Why is it called an **HBCU?**

Uche: HBCUs are historically black colleges and universities that were created before the Civil Rights Act of 1964 to serve African Americans. Schools were segregated, so these institutions allowed people of color to obtain an education.

BJ: Do we have any HBCUs in Houston?

Uche: **Texas Southern University** is considered an HBCU.

Prairie View A&M University is also an HBCU located right outside the city of Houston.

BJ: My old teacher went to **Prairie View A&M University.** He would always talk about this **homecoming** stuff.

Uche: Homecoming is a tradition of welcoming former **alumni** and **professors** back to celebrate the school's history. A majority of schools have a homecoming football game.

BJ: My mom was reading Michelle Obama's book and said she graduated from **Princeton University**. Is that an HBCU as well?
Uche: Princeton University is considered an **Ivy League** school. There is a total of eight **Ivy League** schools. **Ivy League** schools are sometimes viewed as the most prestigious and highly ranked schools in the world.

BJ: You must need a very high **SAT/ACT** and GPA to go to an **Ivy League** school.

Uche: Yes, you do. I have met people with excellent **SAT/ACT** and GPA scores who attend HBCUs as well. You want to attend a **college** that is right for you.

BJ: If I attend **college** far away from home, where will I stay?

Uche: Schools have what are called **dorms** and **student-living apartments**. You will have a bed and a roommate.

BJ: How do students eat?

Uche: They have a dining area, and students go there for breakfast, lunch, and dinner. When I went on a **college** tour at the University of Texas at Austin, I saw that some of their **dorms** had a Wendy's inside. They even have Chick-fil-A on campus.

BJ: I saw Chick-fil-A when I went to visit **Texas Southern University**, too.

Uche: **College** is very fun. Some people say negative things about school, but the more you learn, the more you earn!

BJ: How long is **college**?

Uche: **College** is four years if you are receiving a **bachelor's degree**, and two years if you are receiving an **associate's** degree. Some people attend technical school as well to become **welders or car mechanics**.

BJ: What about people who want to become **doctors** and **lawyers**?

Uche: If you want to become a **doctor** or **lawyer**, you must first obtain your **bachelor's** degree and apply for **graduate school**.

BJ: That is a lot of schools!

Uche: Remember what I said . . . the more you learn, the more you earn!
Doctors and **lawyers** make a lot of money. It's not about the money; it's about doing what you love.

BJ: I love **journalism**. That's why I selected it.

Uche: People sometimes make the mistake of selecting a job or profession because of money and end up hating it. I learned it is very important to choose something you are passionate about.

BJ: I heard someone say students are more likely to graduate from **college** when they major in something they are **passionate** about.

Uche: Do you have any more questions? The bell is going to ring in 30 minutes.
BJ: What are some more things I can do to prepare for **college**?

Uche: You can join school clubs like the student council and the chess team.
BJ: Why does joining school clubs help?

Uche: Colleges like to see students who are active and participating in clubs and having leadership positions also help when they review a student's **resume.**

BJ: What is a **resume?**

Uche: A **resume** shows a person's background, skills, accomplishments, and academic performance.

BJ: How come we don't have **resumes** right now?

Uche: Students normally start building their resumes in middle school.

BJ: Now, I want to run for class president! I never liked participating in after-school clubs. I thought the cool kids never did it.

First and Last Name
Address, City, State, Zip Code
Email Address
Phone Number

Expected Graduation: Month Year

EDUCATION

Your High School, City, State
Classes Taken: *Optional*
Class Rank: *Optional*
SAT Score: / ACT Score: *Optional*
GPA:

Year - Year
Year - Year
Year - Year

AWARDS AND ACHIEVEMENTS

☒ Honor/Achievement #1 (Year)
☒ Honor/Achievement #2 (Year)
☒ Honor/Achievement #3 (Year)
☒ Etc.

Month Year - Month Year

EXTRACURRICULAR ACTIVITIES

Name of Club #1, Position Held (if any)
Name of Club #2, Position Held (if any)
Name of Club #3, Position Held (if any)

Month Year - Month Year

EXPERIENCE

Place of Employment, Title of Position
Include duties you performed

☒ Make each duty a separate bullet point

Place You Volunteered, Title of Position
☒ Include duties performed
☒ Try to have between 2-3 bullet points for each experience listed

SKILLS

☒ Computer Skills: (Ex: JavaScript, Python, Microsoft Office Suite)
☒ Language Skills: (Ex: Fluent in Spanish and French)
☒ Miscellaneous: (Ex: Customer Service, Written and Oral Communication)

Uche: Data shows students that participate in after-school clubs make better grades and earn more money. You can't be cool if you are making bad grades and avoid **extracurricular** activities.

BJ: You are right, Uche! I will start raising my hand and answering questions. I want to show how cool I am.

Uche: BJ, you are my new best friend. You are a leader and not a follower.

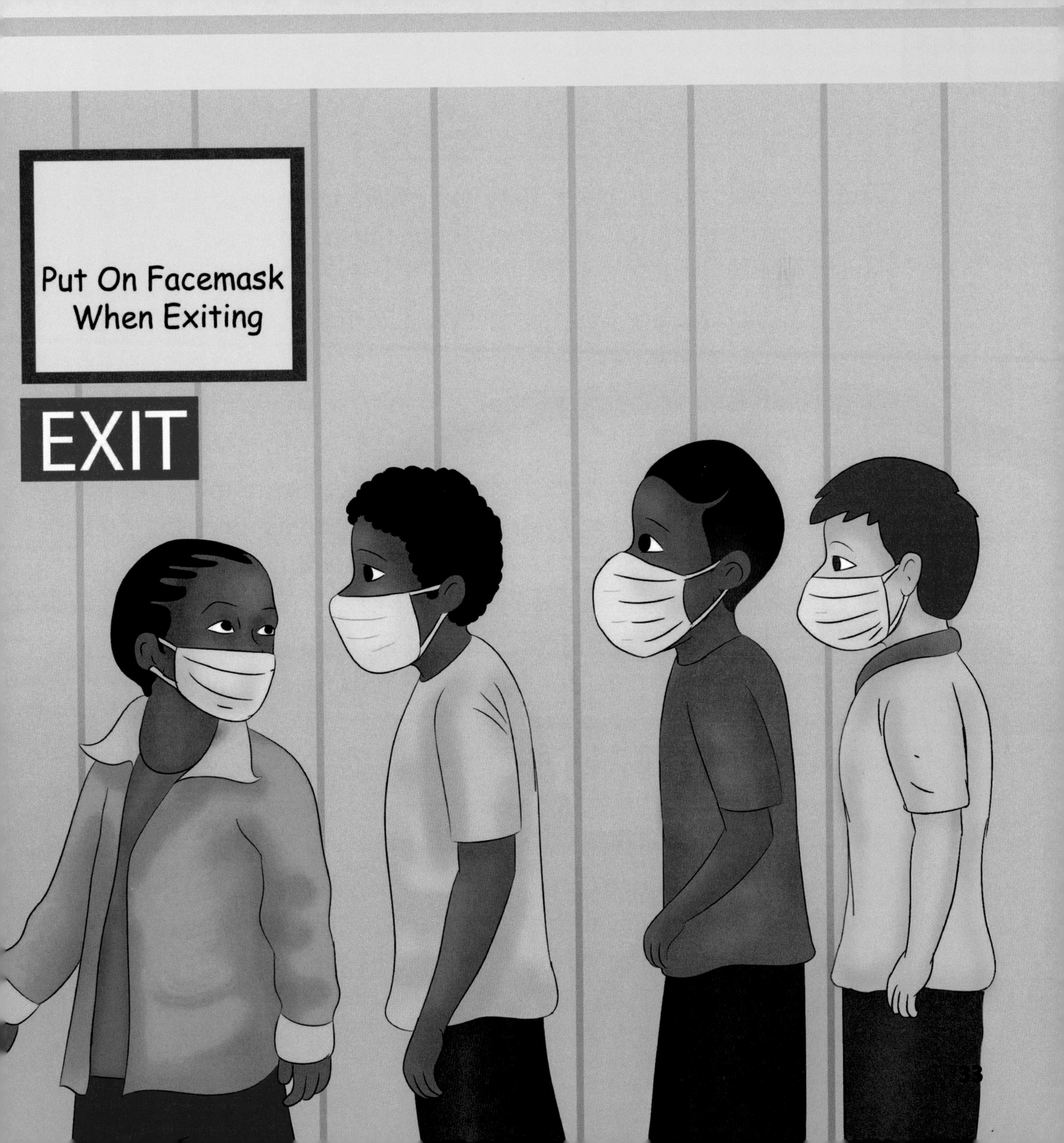
Put On Facemask
When Exiting
EXIT

Keywords Page

- **Diverse**: People are diverse if they come from more than one social, cultural, or economic group, especially members of ethnic or religious minority groups.

- **Doctor**: A doctor is licensed to practice medicine (e.g., physician, surgeon, dentist, or veterinarian).

- **Lawyer**: A lawyer is a professional who represents clients in a court of law. He or she advises or represents clients in other legal matters.

- **ACT**: The ACT is a standardized test used for **college** admissions in the United States. It covers four academic skill areas: English, mathematics, reading, and science reasoning. It also offers an optional direct writing test.

- **SAT**: The Scholastic Assessment Test (SAT) is used for **college** admissions in the United States. The test covers writing, critical reading, and mathematics.

- **College**: A **college** is an institution of higher learning, especially one providing general or liberal arts education rather than technical or professional training.

- **HBCU**: Historically Black Colleges and Universities (HBCUs) are defined by the Higher Education Act of 1965 as "any historically black **college** or university that was established before 1964, whose principal mission was, and is, the education of black Americans, and that is accredited by a nationally recognized accrediting agency or association determined by the Secretary of Education."

- **Texas Southern University**: Texas Southern or TSU is a public historically black university (HBCU) in Houston, Texas.

- **Prairie View A&M**: It is a public historically black university (HBCU) in Prairie View, Texas.

- **Alumni**: Graduate or former students of a specific school, **college**, or university.

- **Professor**: A teacher of the highest academic rank in a **college** or university, who has been awarded the title of professor in a particular branch of learning.

- **Ivy League**: A group of colleges and universities in the northeastern U.S., consisting of Yale, Harvard, Princeton, Columbia, Dartmouth, Cornell, the University of Pennsylvania, and Brown, having a reputation for high scholastic achievement and social prestige.

- **Ineligible**: Not eligible to participate.

- **Dorms**: Places where **college** or university students live.

- **Student-living apartment**: A student apartment is a form of off-campus housing for **college** students. Student apartments are typically not owned by the **college** or university but are available to those enrolled in **college** classes.

- **Journalism**: The occupation of reporting, writing, editing, photographing, or broadcasting news.

- **Bachelor's degree**: A degree given to a student by a **college** or university, usually after four years of study and successfully completing a degree plan.

- **Associate**: This is a degree given to a student who has completed two years of study at a junior **college, college**, or university in the U.S.

- **Welder**: Welding is the process of joining two plastic or metal parts by melting them, with or without using a further molten material.

- **Car Mechanic**: A car mechanic is someone whose occupation is repairing and maintaining automobiles.

- **Graduate School**: Graduate schools award advanced academic degrees with the general requirement that students must already have an undergraduate degree.

- **Passionate**: A passionate individual displays strong feelings or a strong belief in something.

- **Résumé**: A résumé is a formal document used to help people obtain a job.

- **Extracurricular Activities**: These refer to activities pursued outside the classroom. Some examples of extracurricular activities are those organized by sports teams, speech and debate teams, or the student council.

Author's notes

I grew up and attended school in Alief ISD, in Houston, Texas. I did not know much about the importance of having a good GPA and preparing for **college** until my senior year of high school. Attending the University of Texas at Austin changed my life.

I struggled with reading in elementary and middle school. I failed six classes when I was in high school. But look at me now! This could be your story too. I believe you will accomplish great things and be successful in life.

This book is my gift to you. People will tell you that you are not smart. People will sometimes laugh at the clothes you wear and make fun of the way you talk. Keep going! No matter what other people tell you, the world is yours to claim.

What's the biggest lesson? Be a team player and make those around you better.

Let's be great,

Henry Keculah, Jr.

@HenryKeculahjr

#Alief

Made in the USA
Monee, IL
14 September 2020